Traditional Crafts from
JAPAN

Traditional Crafts from
JAPAN

by Florence Temko

with illustrations by Randall Gooch

 Lerner Publications Company • Minneapolis

To Rachel, Perri, David, Dennis, Janet, Tyler, and Yolanda, and for our wish for international peace and friendship.

Over the years, I have tucked away bits of information in my files that have contributed to my fascination with crafts. They were gathered mainly from personal meetings, books, magazines, libraries, and museums in the United States and abroad. I regret it is no longer possible to disentangle these many and varied resources, but I would like to acknowledge gratefully and humbly everyone who has helped to make this book possible.

—Florence Temko

Lerner Publications Company
A division of Lerner Publishing Group
241 First Avenue North
Minneapolis, MN 55401 U.S.A.

Website address: www.lernerbooks.com

Library of Congress Cataloging-in-Publication Data

Temko, Florence.
    Traditional crafts from Japan / by Florence Temko ; with illustrations by Randall Gooch.
        p.   cm. — (Culture crafts)
    Includes bibliographical references and index.
    Summary: Explains the meaning of Japanese culture which is found in eight traditional handicrafts and provides instructions for creating them. Includes a list of materials needed.
    ISBN 0–8225–2938–6 (lib. bdg. : alk. paper)
    1. Handicraft—Japan—Juvenile literature. [1. Handicraft—Japan.] I. Gooch, Randall, ill. II. Title. III. Series.
TT105.T45 2001
745'.0952—dc21   95-46583

Manufactured in the United States of America
1 2 3 4 5 6 – JR – 06 05 04 03 02 01

CONTENTS

WHAT ARE CRAFTS?

All over the world, people need baskets, bowls, clothes, and tools. People now make many of these things in factories. But long ago, people made what they needed by hand. They formed clay and metal pots for cooking. They wove cloth to wear. They made baskets to carry food. We call these things "crafts" when they are made by hand.

Grandparents and parents taught children how to make crafts. While they worked, the elders told stories. These stories told of their family's culture—all of the ideas and customs that a group of people believe in and practice. Children learned these stories as they learned the ways of making crafts. They painted or carved symbols from the stories on their crafts.

6

Year after year, methods and symbols were passed from parents to children. Still, each bowl or basket they made would look a little different. A craft made by hand—even by the same person—never turns out the exact same way twice.

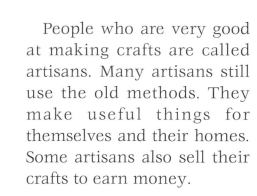

People who are very good at making crafts are called artisans. Many artisans still use the old methods. They make useful things for themselves and their homes. Some artisans also sell their crafts to earn money.

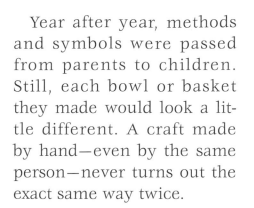

Left to right: A painted tile from Turkey, a Pueblo Indian pitcher, a pot from Peru, and a porcelain dish from China

MATERIALS AND SUPPLIES

Some of the suggested materials for the crafts in this book are the same as those used by Japanese artisans. Others will give you almost the same results. Most materials can be found at home or purchased at local stores. Check your telephone book for stores in your area that sell art materials, craft supplies, and teachers' supplies. Whenever you can, try to use recyclable materials—and remember to reuse or recycle the scraps from your projects.

MEASUREMENTS

Sizes are given in inches. If you prefer to use the metric system, you can use the conversion chart on page 58. Because fractions can be hard to work with, round all metric measurements to the nearest whole number.

FINISHES

The crafts in this book that are made from paper will last longer if you brush or sponge them with a thin coat of finish. These are some choices:

White glue (Elmer's or another brand) is the most widely available. Use it at full strength or dilute it with a few drops of water. Apply it with a brush or small sponge. (The sponge should be thrown away after you use it.) White glue dries clear.

Acrylic medium is sold in art supply stores. It handles much like white glue. You can choose a glossy (shiny) finish or a matte (dull) finish.

JAPANESE CRAFTS

Japan lies in the Pacific Ocean. The Sea of Japan separates the country from the eastern coast of the Asian mainland. Japan consists of a chain of four main islands and several thousand smaller ones.

Throughout the country's history, Japanese people have produced a variety of crafts. Artisans developed exceptional skills in ceramics, woodblock printing, weaving, and papermaking. Japanese clothing, dishes, and other everyday things are often decorated with flowers and animals. The designs are often based on ancient folklore or on nature. For example, flowers that bloom at different times of the year symbolize the four seasons: the peony for spring, the lotus for summer, the chrysanthemum for fall, and plum blossoms for winter. Japanese artisans try to make their practical objects as beautiful as possible. This highly developed sense of artistry is called *shibui.*

Some Japanese villages specialize in only one craft. The people of a town near a good source of clay might make pottery. A group living near a river might produce handmade paper, a process that requires a lot of water. These folk crafts are known as *mingei,* or "the art of the people."

In modern times, as many handmade objects are being replaced with machine-made goods, some Japanese government agencies and private companies provide help for artisans to continue working at their skills. Teachers and parents introduce children to crafts at school and at home, thus passing on age-old traditions to the next generation.

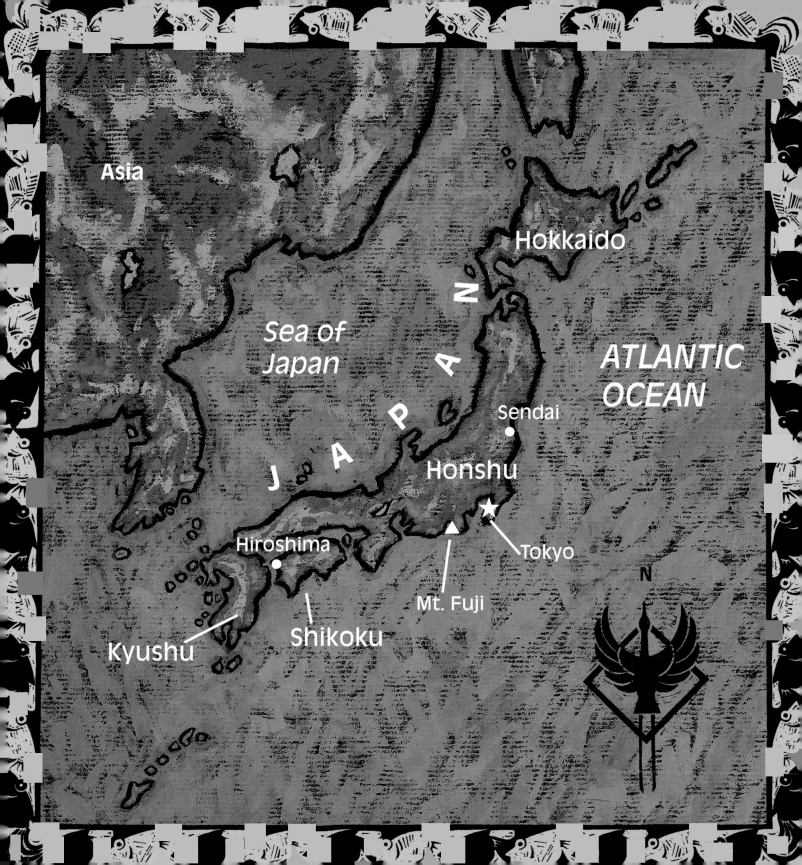

Daruma

Daruma dolls have no legs and appear to be armless, too. But if you look closely, you can see sleeves painted on the front of the body. Japanese people say that the doll is hiding his hands in his sleeves.

DARUMA DOLLS

Round, red *daruma* dolls are very popular in Japan. They represent a monk who sat still and meditated for nine years until he lost the use of his legs. The bodies of some daruma are weighted so that they always bounce upright when they are pushed over. Standing up again and again symbolizes a person's determination to keep trying.

The daruma on sale in shops have two blank white eyes. When they are seen in homes, however, they have one or two eyes painted in. According to custom, a person brings home a daruma, makes a secret wish, and paints a black circle into one eye. The doll receives its other eye only when the wish has been fulfilled.

Dozens of new papier-mâché daruma dolls await painting at a Japanese craft factory (above). An artist decorates each one by hand (left), using traditional colors and designs.

TECHNIQUE

Japanese daruma dolls vary in height from three inches to three feet. Craftspeople make the dolls by molding papier-mâché over a wooden form. Then they paint the dolls in the traditional style.

HOW-TO PROJECT

You can make daruma by covering empty eggshells with papier-mâché. If you weight the bottom of the eggshell, the daruma will always stand upright if it is knocked over.

1 Cover your work area with newspaper. Use the thumbtack to make a pinprick in the wide end of the eggshell and a penny-sized hole in the narrow end. (Hold the egg gently and press the tack carefully but firmly into the eggshell.) Hold the egg over a cup and blow into the small hole until the insides fall into the cup. Wash the eggshell, drain it well, and put a small piece of masking tape over the small pinprick.

You need:

Egg
Thumbtack
Cup
Masking tape
Paperboard strip, ½ inch by
   5½ inches
Five pennies
Library paste, white glue, or
   wallpaper paste
Bowl
White tissue paper, torn into
   2-inch squares
Poster or acrylic paints in red,
   black, and white

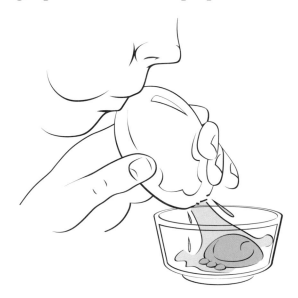

2 Roll the paperboard strip into a circle and tape the ends together. Stand the eggshell in the cardboard circle, with the larger hole pointing down. Pour some paste or glue into a bowl. If necessary, dilute it with some water until it flows like heavy cream. Lay a tissue square on top of the paste to wet it. Plaster the tissue to the top of the eggshell. Cover the top with more gluey tissue squares.

3 Turn the eggshell over. Pour a little paste into it. Drop the pennies into the paste. Then cover the top of the eggshell with gluey tissue squares, covering the hole.

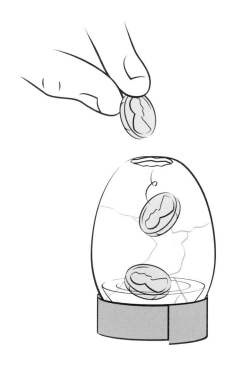

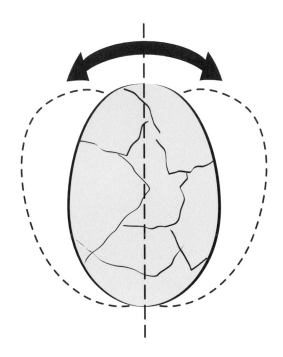

4 Take the egg off the stand and balance the egg so it stands upright. If necessary, gently shake the egg to move the pennies around until the egg balances evenly. Let dry undisturbed for one or two days.

5 Paint the daruma. For a traditional doll, paint the body red, leaving a space for a fierce face with round, empty eyes. On the front, paint the sleeves of the robe.

WHAT ELSE YOU CAN DO

Plastic Eggs: Around Easter, stores carry two-piece plastic eggs that are wonderful substitutes for real eggshells—and you don't have to poke holes in them.

Set a Goal: Japanese people use daruma to mark a new personal or business venture. When you start a new school year or try out for a team, you can paint in one eye of your daruma. The doll reminds you that you need to work hard to achieve your goals. When you succeed, paint in the other eye to celebrate.

Ka-mon

Ka-mon are easy to cut. They make colorful paper decorations.

FAMILY CRESTS

In the A.D. 500s, noble Japanese families began displaying *ka-mon,* or family crests, on their clothing and other possessions. The designs were usually based on flowers, animals, tools, or other things from daily life. Ka-mon were placed on the back, front, and both sleeves of kimonos. In times of war, crests on armor and banners helped soldiers tell friend from foe during battles. In modern times, people use ka-mon for decorations. Cities and businesses adopt crests as logos or trademarks.

TECHNIQUE

Japanese people sometimes cut ka-mon from paper squares, which may be left flat or folded one or more times. People cut folded paper to create symmetrical designs. Very simple cutting may appear quite complicated when the paper is unfolded.

Japanese people display ka-mon on clothing (above) and on banners (right).

HOW-TO PROJECT

Ka-mon can be cut from bond paper, origami squares, or any other kind of thin paper. When cutting curves, keep the hand holding the scissors still and turn the paper with your other hand as you cut. This results in smoother lines.

> **You need:**
>
> Thin paper, cut into squares
> Scissors
> Pencil

1 Fold the paper square according to the pattern you've chosen from page 23.

For the first two designs, fold the paper in half from corner to corner to make a triangle. Fold it in half again to form a smaller triangle. The paper is ready for the interlocking squares design.

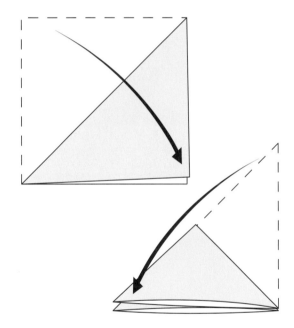

For the flower ka-mon, fold the smaller triangle in half once more.

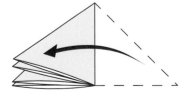

For the starburst, fold a paper square in half to make a rectangle.

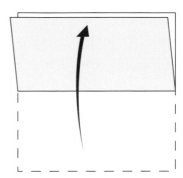

Find the center of the folded edge. To do this, bring the left and right edges of the paper together. Pinch the middle of the folded edge to mark the center. Bend the paper into thirds (without creasing) so that the original folded edge forms a point at the center mark. Wiggle the paper until the two sides overlap each other exactly, then crease.

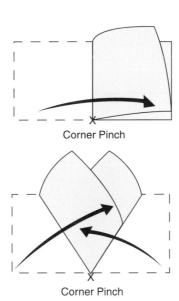

Corner Pinch

Corner Pinch

Aim the folded point toward yourself. Fold the paper in half vertically.

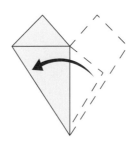

For the five-pointed star, fold the paper in half from edge to edge. With the folded edge toward you, find the middle of the short left edge. Bring the bottom right corner slightly above the mark.

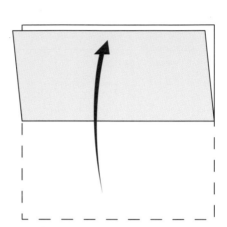

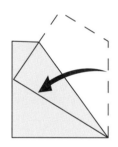

Fold the right edge over to meet the diagonal folded edge.

Fold the left side over. The edges of the paper should be even. Adjust the folds if necessary and crease the paper.

2 Draw one of the designs shown here. Cut on the pencil lines. Unfold the paper carefully.

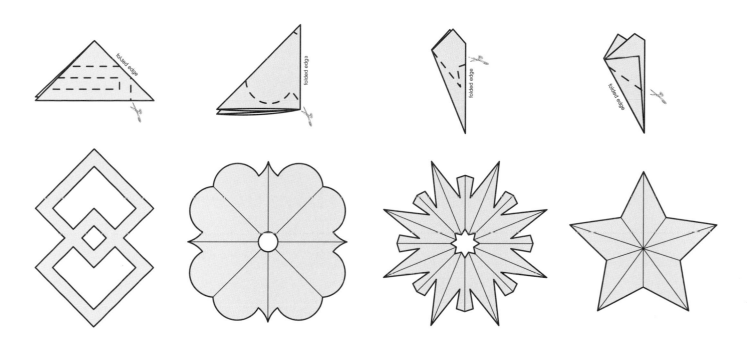

WHAT ELSE YOU CAN DO

Gluing Down: Ka-mon look best when they are placed on a background of another color. First, put a little glue on a piece of scratch paper. Next place the cutout on the background. Use one hand to hold down the middle and lift up one corner. Dip the forefinger of the other hand into the glue. Spread a very thin layer of glue on a small area of the cutout. Press the cutout against the background. Repeat on different areas of the ka-mon until it is all glued down.

Koi Nobori

You can make a koi nobori out of cloth or tissue paper.

FISH WIND SOCKS

On May 5, people all over Japan celebrate Children's Day with fish-shaped wind socks called *koi nobori*. The name means "flying carp," after a kind of fish known for its strength to swim against the stream. Families set up a tall bamboo pole in front of the house. From the pole, they fly a koi nobori for each child. The topmost and largest one is dedicated to the oldest child and the lower, smaller wind socks to the younger children. As the breeze blows, the wind socks seem to swim in the air like

Outside a Japanese home, a school of koi nobori flutters in the breeze.

The traditional koi nobori pattern shows the fish's mouth, its head with large eyes, its scaly body, and its flowing fins.

fish in water. Koi nobori represent a wish that the children be healthy and strong, like the carp.

TECHNIQUE

Carp wind socks are simple to make from fabric or paper. Most are painted in a traditional style. They were originally made by hand, but in modern times, most are made in factories.

HOW-TO PROJECT

You can cut a flying carp from inexpensive fabric. Depending on the fabric's width, half a yard will give you enough material for two or three wind socks.

1 Cut a 20- by 18-inch piece of fabric. Fold it in half the short way. Draw a fish pattern onto the fabric. Cut on the pencil lines.

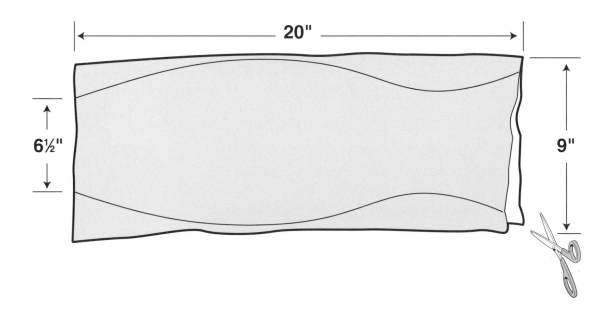

2 Sew or glue the two pieces together at the top and bottom edges. Leave the mouth and tail ends open.

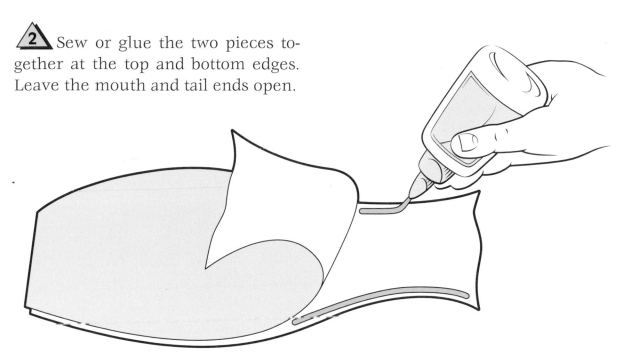

3 Cut a piece of cardboard 1 inch wide by 13 inches long. Roll it into a circle. Adjust it to fit around the inside of the mouth. Staple the narrow ends of the cardboard together.

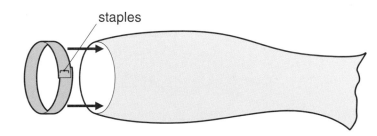

staples

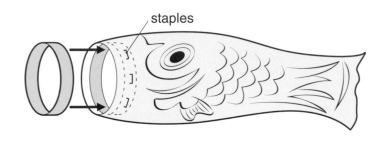

staples

4 Slide the cardboard ring into the fish's mouth. Fold an inch of fabric over the ring. Staple through the cloth and the cardboard about $\frac{1}{2}$ inch from the outside edge. On both sides of the windsock, paint the traditional design or make up your own pattern.

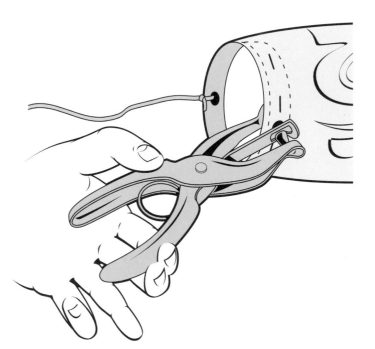

5 Punch a hole through the cloth and the cardboard ring on either side of the fish's mouth. Tie the ends of a 15-inch piece of string to the two holes. Use another piece of string to tie the carp to a pole or tree.

WHAT ELSE YOU CAN DO

Paper: Instead of fabric, you can make a flying carp from tissue paper.

Birthday Parties: A wind sock makes a nice birthday gift for a friend, or all the guests at a birthday party can make their own.

Wall Decoration: A fish without the cardboard ring can be hung as a wall decoration.

Maneki Neko

The cat holds its paw in the position that Japanese people use to beckon others. The person holds the palm and fingers downwards and draws the hand backwards. Japanese customers imagine the cat calling them and their money into shops.

WELCOMING CAT

Some Japanese stores and restaurants display a *maneki neko*—a figurine of a cat with one paw raised in welcome. The cats became popular about two hundred years ago because of two competing restaurants. One restaurant had started displaying a golden cat, and the other had a silver cat. The two businesses attracted many customers. Since then other merchants, as well as ordinary people, have adopted the cat as a good luck symbol for success and wealth.

The maneki neko on the left are painted in the common black and brown spot pattern.

Sometimes maneki neko are shown holding a coin for good luck. You can mold a coin of clay and attach it to your cat sculpture while both pieces are wet. Paint the coin gold or silver when the project is dry.

TECHNIQUE

Craftspeople make a maneki neko from clay, either by hand or in a mold. Most cats are painted with yellow eyes, red ears, and brown and black spots on a white background. They may also be coated in gold or silver, just like the original figures.

HOW-TO PROJECT

Most kinds of clay, except modeling clay, can be used to make the cat. Always prepare the clay according to the directions on the package. It is important to join pieces of clay with water. Pieces that are not moistened will separate when drying. First dampen both pieces where they are to be joined and then press the pieces together. Wet your finger or a tool and smooth the joint.

You need:

Newspaper to protect your
    work area
Plastic wrap
Self-hardening or other clay
Poster or acrylic paints
Paintbrush
Paper towels
Bowl of water

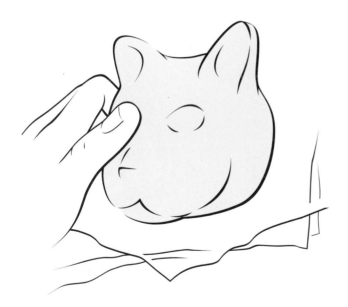

1 Cover your work area with layers of newspaper. Put a piece of plastic wrap on top. For the cat's head, roll a lump of clay into a ball about 3 inches across. Shape two small lumps of clay into ears and join them to the smaller ball. Pinch the ears and face to look like a cat.

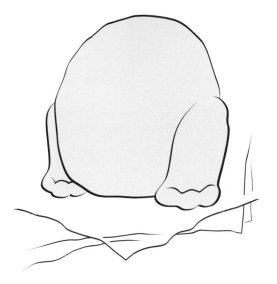

2 For the body, roll a ball measuring about 4 inches across. For the back legs, roll a pair of 1-inch balls. Flatten each 1-inch ball and pinch an edge to make a foot. Attach the back legs to the body.

3 Roll a sausage and shape it into the front leg with the welcoming paw. Join the head and leg to the body. Roll two sausages, one for the other front leg and one for the tail. Attach them. Let the figure dry.

4 When the clay is dry, paint the cat in traditional colors or however you like.

Origami Crane

According to Japanese folklore, cranes live for a hundred years or more. They symbolize good wishes for a long life and often appear on clothes, paintings, and greeting cards. An ancient legend says that if someone folds a thousand paper cranes, his or her wish will be granted.

PAPER FOLDING

When paper was first introduced in Japan in the A.D. 500s, it was given as a valuable present. Later, folded paper ornaments became part of religious ceremonies. Paper folding, or origami, developed into a pastime and spread to many countries of the world. In Japan children learn to fold squares of paper into birds, hats, flowers, fish, and anything else imaginable. A large bird called a crane is one of the best-known origamis.

A pair of girls fold cranes and other origami figures (above). Paper folders from around the world send bundles of a thousand origami cranes to hang at Hiroshima Peace Memorial Park (right). The monument commemorates the people who died when U.S. forces dropped an atomic bomb on the city of Hiroshima, Japan, in 1945 at the end of World War II.

TECHNIQUE

People use special paper, brightly colored on one side and white or colored on the other, for origami. According to the rules of origami, the paper must be folded without any cutting or gluing. A beginner may fold a duck with only five creases, but an expert paper folder can create a dinosaur that requires hundreds of creases. Many designs begin with exactly the same folds. From then on, the project could become a boat, a star, a bird, or any number of other designs.

HOW-TO PROJECT

You can use origami paper from a craft supply store, or you can cut other kinds of thin paper into squares.

1 If paper is colored on one side only, begin with the colored side up. Fold the square on the diagonal from corner to corner. Unfold the crease. Fold on the other diagonal. Unfold and turn the paper over.

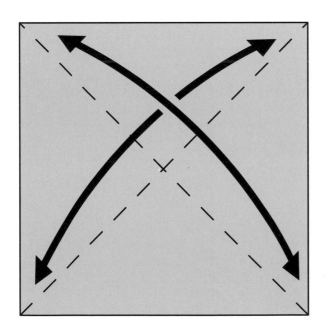

△2 Fold the paper in half, edge to edge. Unfold. Fold the paper in half the other way, but this time do not unfold.

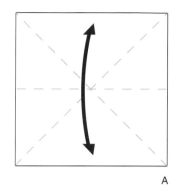

A

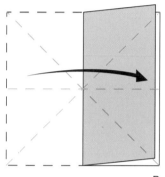

B

△3 Hold the paper with the open edges pointing up. Bring the top corners together so that the paper bends on the diagonal creases.

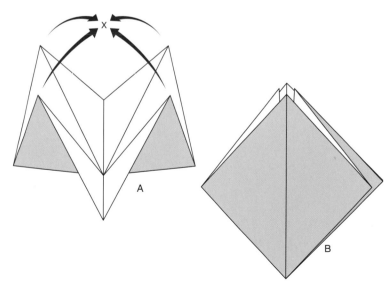

A

B

4 Place the paper flat on the table. You should have two flaps on each side. If you have three flaps on one side and one on the other, flip over one flap.

Place the paper so that the top corner is closed, but the bottom is open. On the front, fold the top flaps to the middle so that the bottom edges touch the center. Turn the paper over and repeat the step on the back. Your paper should be kite-shaped.

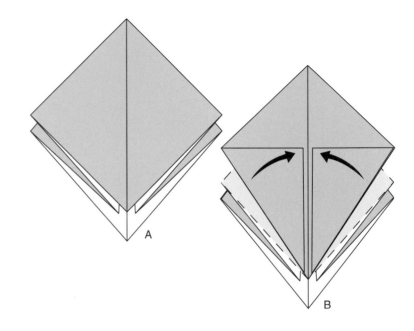

5 Fold the top triangle down, and then fold it up again. Turn the paper over and repeat this step. The paper looks the same as before but has an added crease, X-Y.

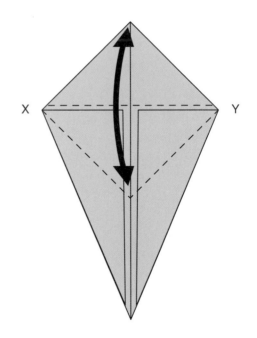

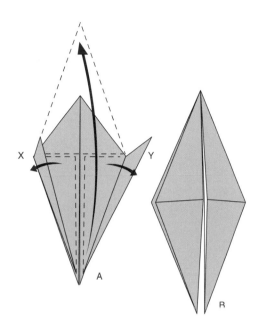

6 Open the front flaps slightly. Lift the bottom corner up so that it folds back on the crease X-Y. The paper looks like a bird's beak during this step. Fold the corner all the way back so that it is flat on the table. The edges will fold in on the side creases, and the paper will look like a diamond. Turn the paper over and repeat on the back.

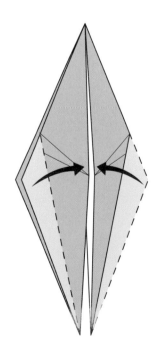

7 Fold the bottom part of the flaps so that the outer edges touch the center of the paper. Turn the paper over and repeat. Your paper looks like a skinny diamond.

8 Fold the two long "legs" up on the two short dotted lines and unfold. Turn back the top flap on one side of the paper. Fold the leg backward on the creases you just made. Close the top flap. Repeat on the other side. The paper should look like a crown with two skinny points and a wide point.

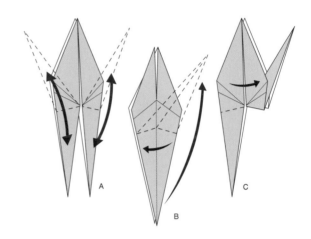

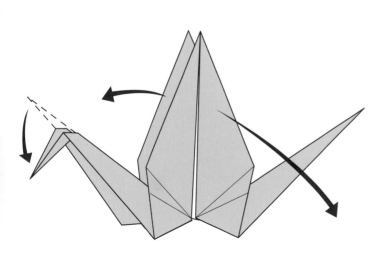

9 Choose one skinny point to be the head. Bend the point down and crease. Turn the paper so the head faces you. Gently bend down the left and right sides of the wide point. These are the wings. Inflate the body by blowing into the hole at the bottom. If this doesn't work, hold the crane so the head points down. Gently tug on both wings, first downward and then upward, until the crane's back flattens.

WHAT ELSE YOU CAN DO

Papers: Use giftwrap, stationery, magazine pages, or waste paper.

Hanging Crane: Hang colorful cranes in windows or around your room. Fold the crane completely and then unfold it to step 4. Knot one end of a piece of thread to a button. Thread the other end through a needle and push it through the middle of the crane. Then refold the crane.

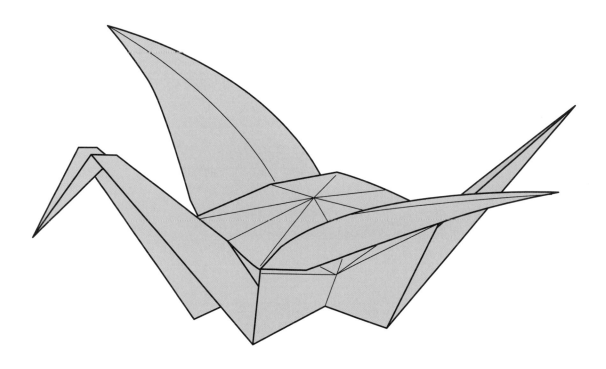

Stenciled Fabrics

Simple patterns stand out from the dyed backgrounds of these stenciled fabric squares.

PASTE-RESIST STENCILING

Japanese clothing is often decorated with a special kind of stenciling called paste-resist. This process of dyeing fabrics began in the 1600s as an inexpensive imitation of the woven fabrics that wealthy people wore. The patterns range from simple stripes to pictures of fish, flowers, and many other designs.

Paste-resist stenciled designs can be plain (above) or very fancy and detailed (above left).

TECHNIQUE

Japanese craftspeople cut stencils from handmade paper. The stencils are very strong and may be used over and over again. To prepare a cloth for dyeing, an artisan places a stencil on a piece of plain cloth and covers it with rice-flour paste. The artisan removes the stencil from the fabric, but the paste remains. The same stencil may be placed several times on the same piece of fabric to pattern a whole length of material. The person dyes the cloth—most often in dark blue—but the areas soaked with paste do not absorb the color. When the dye has set, the craftsperson washes the cloth, and the paste dissolves.

HOW-TO PROJECT

This project shows how to pattern a piece of fabric with the paste-resist method.

Caution: This craft may be messy, so wear old clothes and cover your work area with newspaper. Make sure an adult helps you with steps 3 and 4.

1 Cut a stencil from a shopping bag, using one of the patterns on page 47. Unfold the paper and place it on the fabric.

You need:

Old newspapers
Cotton muslin fabric pieces,
    6 inches by 5 inches
A shopping bag
Pencil
Scissors
Disposable plastic cup
White glue
Dye (liquid or powder)
Stiff paintbrush
White tissue paper

2 Make sure the edges of the stencil are close to the fabric at all times. Using the glue bottle like a pencil, trace the outline of the stencil. With your forefinger, spread the glue from the outside lines toward the center of the traced spaces. Add more glue as needed to cover the design, and rub the glue well into the fabric. Remove the stencil and let the fabric dry.

3 In the plastic cup, prepare the dye according to the directions on the package. The darker you make your dye, the better your stencil will look. Using a light touch, brush the dye over the fabric. Let the fabric dry on newspaper. Always wipe off any drips of dye anywhere right away.

4 Rinse the fabric in cold water and rub off the glue. Some dye may also bleed off. Let the fabric dry. You may want to ask an adult to place the finished fabric between two pieces of tissue paper and iron it for you.

WHAT ELSE YOU CAN DO

Greeting Cards: Glue your fabric square to a piece of folded paper to make a card.

Other Patterns: You can create other designs with different stencil cutouts. On larger pieces of fabric you can repeat any design several times.

Clothing: Sew your squares to T-shirts, vests, skirts, or other clothes. Or try stenciling right on clothing. Put a thick layer of newspapers between layers of fabric to prevent glue or dye from bleeding through.

Flower pattern:

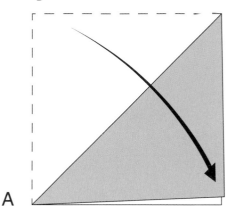

A

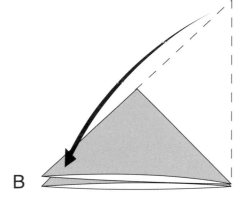

B

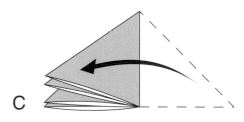

C

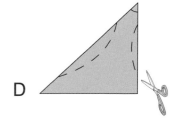

D

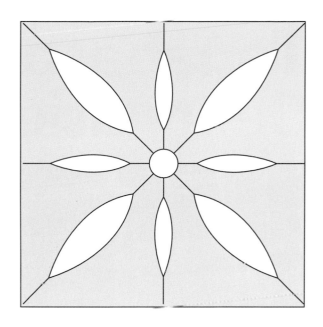

Tanabata Festival Decorations

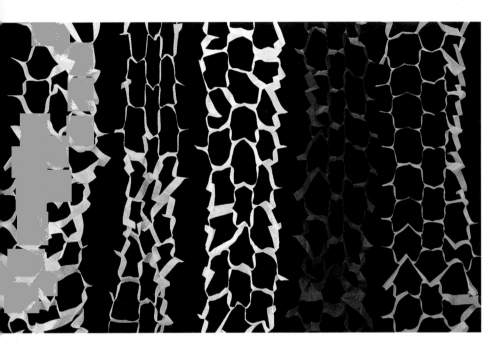

The paper decorations called tanabata are a snap to cut, and they add a festive air to any celebration.

PAPER NETTING

On July 7 of each year, Japanese people display paper decorations called *tanabata*. The cut paper ornaments represent pieces of weaving. The holiday celebrates a legend about a weaver princess and a cowherder who were stars in the sky and the birds who helped them.

Orihime (oh-ree-HEE-may) was weaving a piece of cloth to make a coat for her father, the king of the sky, when she fell in love with a cowherder named Hikoboshi (hee-koh-BOH-shee). Because

The town of Sendai holds the biggest tanabata celebration in Japan. Once a year, citizens parade elaborate floats, huge banners, and spectacular paper lanterns through the streets. Many tourists join the celebration, and it is shown on Japanese television.

the pair spent every possible hour together, Orihime forgot about her weaving, which annoyed the king. In punishment he sent Orihime and Hikoboshi to live at opposite ends of the Milky Way. Finally he permitted them to meet on one day of the year. There was only one problem: How were they to meet even on that day without a bridge across the Milky Way? Fortunately the birds of the sky loved the princess and offered to make a bridge with their outspread wings.

TECHNIQUE

Tanabata designs vary, as people cut paper however they like. People attach the decorations to long bamboo poles. Then they make wishes for good luck or for improving skills such as weaving. In another custom, young people write romantic love poems on strips of colored paper.

HOW-TO PROJECT

The directions show how to cut paper netting.

You need:

Tissue paper, 15 inches by
    10 inches
Scissors

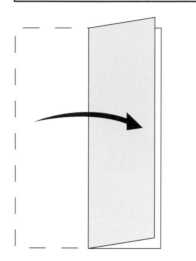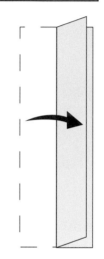

1 Fold the tissue paper in half lengthwise. Fold it in half again.

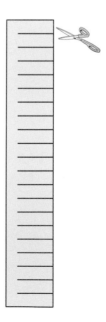

2 Make parallel cuts across the paper about ¾ inch apart. Begin the cuts at one long edge and stop about ½ inch from the opposite edge.

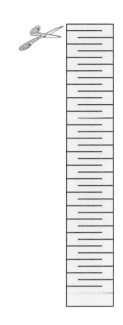

3 From the opposite side, cut in between the slits you have just made. Leave about ½ inch uncut.

4 Place the paper on a flat surface and carefully unfold it. Pull the ends of the netting to open the cuts.

PULL

PULL

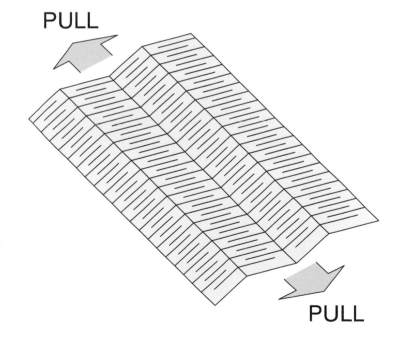

WHAT ELSE YOU CAN DO

Room Decorations: On July 7, or for any celebration, you can decorate a room with tanabata cuttings. Use bigger sheets of tissue for decorating a large room or auditorium. The netting can be carried while folded flat and strung up quickly.

Den-Den Daiko

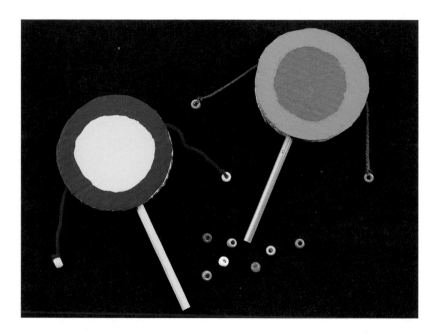

Den-den daiko are festive, noisy toys.

TAIKO

Japanese musicians play many different kinds of drums. One kind is the *taiko,* or "fat drum." Taiko may have been used in Japan for more than two thousand years. These drums come in many sizes, from one to six feet across or even bigger. Musicians play them with sticks.

Japanese children enjoy a tiny toy drum called *den-den daiko.* (When the word *taiko* is used in a two-part word, the T sound changes into a D.) Unlike their giant cousins, den-den daiko are only a few inches across. The brightly colored toys are easy to play, and people often buy them for festivals and celebrations.

TECHNIQUE

To make a den-den daiko, the craftsperson mounts a wooden cylinder on a stick. On each end of the drum, the artisan stretches a thin leather skin over the opening and tacks it in place. He or she uses string to attach beaters to either side of the toy.

To play the den-den daiko, a person holds the stick between the palms and rubs the hands back and forth. The string beaters strike the drumheads rhythmically.

The earliest taiko may have been used in war. Officers probably drummed out signals to their soldiers as they fought. The thunderous sound of the large drums would have been easy to hear over the noise of the battle.

Later in Japan's history, taiko became instruments in the highly cultured music of the emperor's court. Priests also played the drums in religious music, which they performed at temples. Since the 1950s, taiko have become popular instruments for amateur and folk musicians in Japan and around the world.

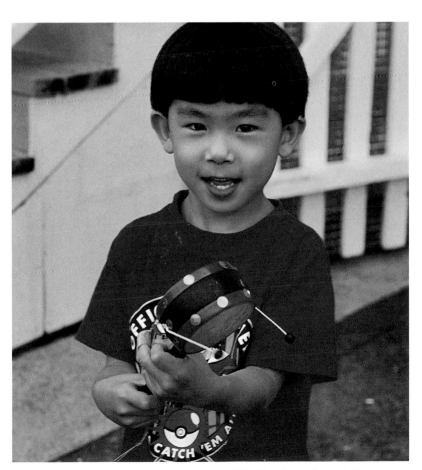

A Japanese-American boy plays with his den-den daiko.

HOW-TO PROJECT

1 Place one of the cardboard circles plain side down. Tape one piece of yarn to either side of the circle.

> **You need:**
>
> Two 4-inch circles of corrugated cardboard
> Clear or masking tape
> Two 5-inch lengths of yarn or string
> Eight 1-inch squares of corrugated cardboard
> White glue
> New, unsharpened pencil
> Two beads
> Poster or acrylic paints

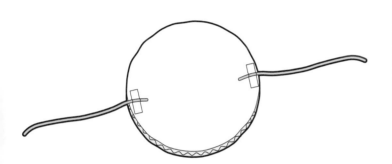

2 Peel one layer of paper off a cardboard square and glue the square, ridged side up, to the center of the circle. The long side of the ridges should run parallel to the sides of your drum.

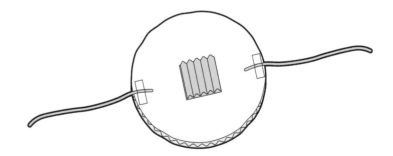

3 Put some glue in the bottom of one of the ridges. Lay the pencil onto the glue.

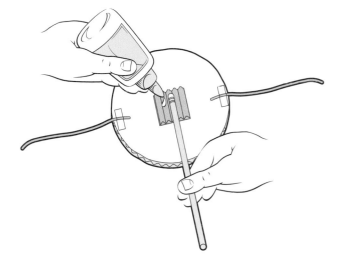

4 Put some more glue on top of the pencil. Peel another cardboard square and lay it, ridged side down, on top of the pencil.

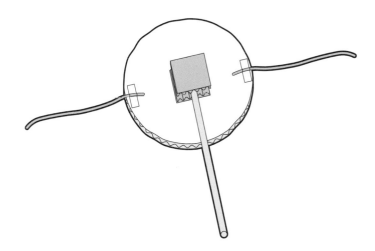

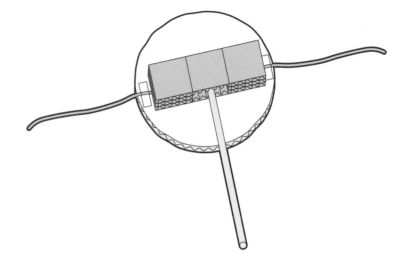

⑤ Glue a stack of three cardboard squares on either side of the pencil.

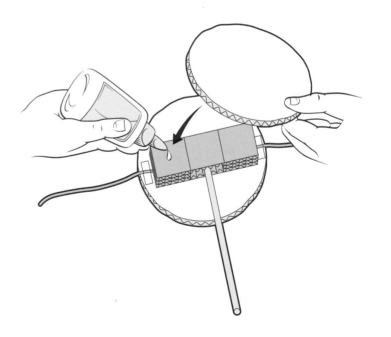

⑥ Spread a little glue on the stacks and on the center cardboard square. Set the second cardboard circle in place, keeping its edges even with the first circle. Let the glue dry.

7 Tie a bead to the end of each piece of yarn. Be sure the beads hang evenly when you hold up the drum. Trim the extra yarn away. Paint your drum.

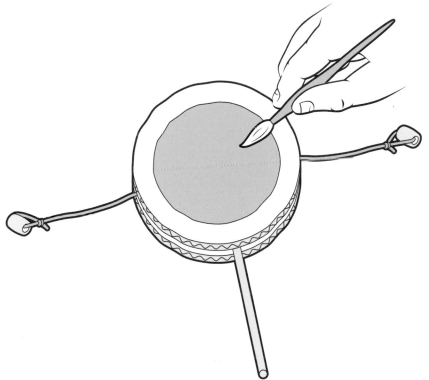

WHAT ELSE YOU CAN DO

Noisemakers: Make a den-den daiko for every guest at a birthday party. When the birthday person blows out the candles, celebrate with lots of noise! Or bring some den-den daiko to a sporting event and use them to cheer for your favorite team.

METRIC CONVERSION CHART

If you want to use the metric system, convert measurements using the chart on the right. Because fractions can be hard to work with, round all metric measurements to the nearest whole number.

when you know:	multiply by:	to find:
Length		
inches	25.00	millimeters
inches	2.54	centimeters
feet	30.00	centimeters
feet	.30	meters
yards	.91	meters
miles	1.61	kilometers
Volume		
teaspoons	5.00	milliliters
tablespoons	15.00	milliliters
fluid ounces	30.00	milliliters
cups	0.24	liters
pints	0.47	liters
quarts	0.95	liters
gallons	3.80	liters
Weight		
ounces	28.00	grams
pounds	0.45	kilograms

GLOSSARY

artisan: A person who is very skilled at making crafts

ceramics: The art of creating objects from baked clay

crest: A symbol that is associated with a family or clan and its history

folklore: Traditional stories, sayings, and customs that are passed down from generation to generation

kimono: A traditional Japanese robe

origami: The art of folding paper into the shapes of animals, plants, and objects

papier-mâché: Torn or shredded paper mixed with glue

stenciling: The process of making designs by laying a cutout over material, applying a coloring, and removing the cutout. The open areas of the cutout receive the color, and the solid areas remain uncolored. In paste-resist stenciling, the coloring is replaced with a paste. After stenciling, the material is dyed. The paste-covered parts of the material stay uncolored, and the parts without paste absorb the dye.

symmetrical: Appearing the same on opposite sides

READ MORE ABOUT JAPAN

Fiction & Folktales

Bodkin, Odds. *The Crane Wife.* San Diego: Harcourt Brace, 1998.

Coerr, Eleanor. *Sadako and the Thousand Paper Cranes.* New York: Puffin, 1999.

Haugaard, Erik, and Masako Haugaard. *The Story of Yuriwaka: A Japanese Odyssey.* Niwot, CO: R. Rinehart Publishers, 1991.

Marton, Jirina. *Lady Kaguya's Secret.* Toronto/New York: Annick Press, 1997.

Quayle, Eric. *The Shining Princess and Other Japanese Legends.* New York: Arcade Publishing, Inc., 1989.

Say, Allen. *Tree of Cranes.* Boston: Houghton Mifflin Co., 1991.

Watkins, Yoko Kawashima. *Tales from the Bamboo Grove.* New York: Bradbury Press, 1992.

Nonfiction

Finley, Carol. *Art of Japan: Wood-Block Color Prints.* Minneapolis: Lerner Publications Company, 1998.

Haskins, Jim. *Count Your Way Through Japan.* Minneapolis: Carolrhoda Books, Inc., 1987.

Littlefield, Holly. *Colors of Japan.* Minneapolis: Carolrhoda Books, Inc., 1997.

Streissguth, Tom. *Japan.* Globe-trotters Club. Minneapolis: Carolrhoda Books, Inc., 1997.

Temko, Florence. *Origami Magic.* New York: Scholastic Inc., 1993.

Weston, Reiko. *Cooking the Japanese Way.* Minneapolis: Lerner Publications Company, 1983.

INDEX

ABOUT THE AUTHOR

Florence Temko is an internationally known author of more than 40 books on world folk crafts and paper arts, including the six books in the Culture Crafts series. She has traveled in 31 countries, gaining much of her skill firsthand. Ms. Temko shows her enthusiasm for crafts through simple, inventive adaptations of traditional arts and crafts projects. She has presented hundreds of hands-on programs in schools and museums, including the Metropolitan Museum of Art in New York City, and at many education conferences across the country and on television. She lives in San Diego, California.

ACKNOWLEDGMENTS

The photographs in this book are reproduced through the courtesy of:

Turkish Republic, Ministry of Culture and Tourism, p. 6 (left); Wilford Archaeology Laboratory, University of Minnesota, by Kathy Raskob/IPS, p. 6 (right); Nelson-Atkins Museum, Kansas City, Missouri, p. 7 (left); Freer Gallery of Art, Smithsonian Institution, p. 7 (right); IPS, pp. 8, 9, 12, 18, 24, 30, 34, 42, 48, 52; Cameramann International, Ltd., pp. 13 (both), 19 (both), 35 (both), 43 (right); Paul J. Buklarewicz, pp. 25, 31, 43 (left), 53 (both); Japan National Tourist Organization, p. 49.

Front cover photograph by IPS.

The map on page 11 is by John Erste. The illustrations on pages 2, 11, 25, and 31 are by Laura Westlund.